Steps on How to Create Wealth from Nothing:

How to Build and Maintain Your Wealth

By

Alexander Blake

scanned, faxed, or retained without approval from the publisher.

Table of contents

INTRODUCTION

Picturing the way you need to stay and what you'd like to perform can assist pressure your economic choices. We'll speak your dreams and aspirations that will help you pick out wealth techniques that meet your needs.

Together we'll clarify your goals to:

Create wealth: Begin your adventure by making money via your business, job, inheritance, or different ventures.

Grow your wealth: Pursue capacity asset boom with a wealth plan primarily based totally on your dreams and emotions closer to risk.

Protect your wealth: Help protect yourself and your family against the unexpected.

Make an impact. Direct your property towards the humans and reasons that are counted maximum to you.

Chapter 1

The components for powerful cash management

I don't claim to be an expert, but I do give some fundamental techniques for wise wealth management along with a set of seven guiding principles that capture my broader worldview.

1. Having wealth entails responsibilities

You are first and predominantly responsible to yourself. If that sounds egotistical, it isn't. You wish to avoid burdening other people. To be financially comfortable for retirement, in the opinion of one family wealth expert I've spoken with, is the best present you can offer your kids.

After that, it becomes a matter of who else, when, and how you are financially accountable. What and who matters to you? Community, which I see as a set of concentric circles with family at the center, followed by those who have supported me, and finally local and larger communities, is the answer for me.

2. Having wealth is a tool of choice

For some people, wealth has varied meanings. I regard it as a treasure trove of worth and potential. You may buy flexibility in your decisions about your education, profession, and way of life with money.

There are always several options available to you. Whatever decision you make, it will either eliminate some possibilities or create new ones that you hadn't considered. Perhaps while your destination may not be quite what you had in mind, you'll probably be happy with it or perhaps pleasantly surprised.

3. Virtuous decisions necessitate virtues

In their broadest sense, objectives represent a vision for your future. They can offer a framework for decision-making, but they are challenging to establish because life is made up of several interconnected domains, including self, family, community, and career. There must be trade-offs; although many refer to it as balance, it's more like juggling. Consider the different aspects of life like balls you are juggling. Which balls are made of crystal and break easily when dropped? Which ones are made of rubber and will bounce, maybe landing in your lap? Financial aspirations are likely to bounce; relationships are more likely to be the crystal balls.

4. The stool has three legs.

I see a three-legged stool for wealth growth, preservation, and transfer, with goals as one of the legs. The other two are people and structure. You have several options for structuring your assets, depending on your objectives. Cash, real estate, stocks, life insurance, pensions, 401(k) plans, holding structures, private foundations, limited partnerships, and more are among the available options. Each has a wide variety of flavors, and many individuals are willing to assist.

Let's use trusts as an illustration. The fundamental queries for the trustor are: Whom do I want to get what? By when? What is my tax payment threshold? However, addressing those questions can become quite complex very quickly.

Depending on their objectives and features, trusts come in a wide variety of forms and names. The fact that laws differ from state to state adds even more intricacy. Then, even for a basic trust, there is still a difficult decision to be made: who should be named as a trustee, and to what extent?

I prefer to appoint friends as trustees whose opinions I value. In addition to appointing one of my sons as an administrative trustee, I have also formed a board of overseers, whose only authority is to remove a trustee and appoint a new one in the event of a problem.

5. Scorecards are crucial

How are you going to quantify your financial success? The focus of many is net income. That is completely incorrect in my opinion because it makes no mention of costs or longevity. A more helpful statistic is the margin (for instance, expenses minus revenues), which shows you whether you are overspending. When you account for the balance sheet implications of depreciation and asset appreciation, debt financing for purchases, and after-tax cash flow, net worth is significantly higher. I keep tabs on my net worth as an individual and as a household.

6. Now is the moment

I usually think of money in terms of quanta, where necessities and wants are divided into separate stages. Early on, it's about having access to enough food, a roof over your head, and education for your kids. Later on, as your assets grow, you buy a house and get access to progressively larger toys and sweets.

The crucial query at hand is: How much is enough?

It increases in difficulty as you go through the phases since you grow accustomed to being comfortable, but it also depends on where you start. It's usually useless to compare oneself to other people. Internal standards are the most crucial. You must determine for yourself what to do once you've reached your objective and how much is enough.

7. If you don't prepare, you prepare to fail.

Benjamin Franklin and Winston Churchill are credited with coining that proverb. In addition,

Dwight D. Eisenhower said, "Preparation is everything; plans are nothing. I concur that the process of preparing is more important than the final product.

Will I have the freedom to do as I like in a year, three years, or five years? Which period ought I to apply? Do I save too little and spend too much? Who could I need to assist? Who can I depend upon to help me? If—or rather, when—my wants or circumstances alter, what will I do?

Organizing aids in addressing those inquiries. It necessitates strategic thinking that is tempered with tactical realism. It's also important for you to accept reality as it is. Understanding your financial situation—what you own, how much you spend, and how much you make—is essential.

Chapter 2

Ways to make money out of nothing

It could seem "mission impossible" to learn how to create wealth from nothing, especially if you have always thought that affluent people either inherit their wealth or have benefited from powerful connections.

A Wealth-X analysis from 2019 revealed that, in reality, 67.7% of the world's ultra-wealthy population—those with $30 million or more in assets—were self-made.

The quick ascent of this ultra-rich class is even more intriguing. The number of ultra-wealthy people climbed from 265,490 in the 2019 report to 290,720 in the 2020 report, a nearly 10% increase.

Two things are clear from the aforementioned data: first, riches may be created out of nothing; and second, the number of people doing the "impossible" is rising.

We beg you to explore the various methods of creating wealth from nothing, rather than daydreaming about the fortune you wish you had inherited.

We'll look at some concrete measures in this article that you can work on right now to start creating wealth from nothing and move toward a more financially independent existence.

Before we begin, consider this: according to T. Harv Eker, writer of Secrets of the Millionaire Mind, "Negative humans need to be wealthy, however wealthy humans are devoted to being wealthy.

You may start to tell the difference right now between commitment and simple desire, which is a crucial distinction.

1. Get knowledge about finances

The first thing that must constantly shift to make any significant changes in our lives is our thinking.

According to business mogul and Rich Dad, Poor Dad author

Robert Kiyosaki, "Everyone can build a financial ark to survive and prosper in the future. However, to assemble an ark with a robust foundation, you need to commit time to your economic education.

Hence, devoting time to your financial education is the first step towards creating riches out of nothing. Learn to understand keywords such as earnings, costs, net worth, ROI, passive income, and financial freedom, among others.

Read books, listen to podcasts and interviews, enroll in courses, and follow blogs like Sarwa's that discuss financial education.

Remember that, similar to all forms of education, financial education needs to be an ongoing endeavor. Continue to learn.

But in this case, care is advised. There is a lot of false information out there as a result of the democratization of financial data.

Make sure you only follow respectable blogs that will point you in the direction of resources from dependable and prosperous business owners, investors, and financial experts.

2. Get a steady source of income

Without a steady stream of income, it is difficult to create riches from nothing. Without saving money, you cannot invest, and without a steady salary, you cannot save.

This means that multilevel marketing, Ponzi schemes, or gambling do not help people create lasting wealth.

Acknowledge and disregard those who tout easy ways to get rich fast, like working three hours a week to accumulate wealth. The source of sustainable wealth is long-term value creation. You can't generate sustainable wealth if you're not producing goods or services with intrinsic worth and making money from them.

Thus, if you don't already have a job, find one now, and if you do, hold onto it.

If you run a small company, keep your attention on adding additional long-term value. According to self-development guru Brian Tracy, "all wealth comes from adding value," which involves creating a company plan one able to "produce more in a faster, better, cheaper, and much less complex manner than someone else.

3. Set up a budget
Explain a budget:

Budget is the vital component of your financial management and planning is a budget. In essence, it accounts for all of your income and expenses, makes sure you set aside funds as needed, and guarantees you have enough money at the end of each pay period.

However, a good budget is much more than that. It enables you to set spending priorities so that you only purchase necessities. Using a budget, you may anticipate your monthly income and prepare for major expenses such as Christmas, school uniforms, or late payments. It provides you with the means to create and realize your aspirations. It forces you to save money so that you can withstand financial shocks and provide a safety net for your family.

Families and people require cash flow planning, just like businesses do. You must create a budget if you hope to achieve actual financial freedom.

Making and following a budget is essential if you want to learn how to create riches out of nothing. You now want to broaden a budget, frequently set on a month-to-month basis, to take the rate of the way your cash has spent the usage of the steady sales supply we simply discussed.

A budget is a financial plan that includes projected income and expenses for a given time. Every household and/or person must establish a monthly budget to determine their anticipated income and estimated expenses. Living without a set budget is like trying to navigate the financial world without a map, and you can be sure that you'll end up lost in the mists of money.

A well-liked method for budgeting is the 50:30:20 rule. With this method, you can create a budget whereby 50% of your income is allocated to necessities such as housing, utilities, food, and medical care, 30% is used for non-essentials such as entertainment, travel, and shopping, and 20% is set aside for savings and investments.

Chapter 3

Why budgeting is important?

One important cause is that via means of information the way you spend your money, it's less difficult to perceive The matters that may be cut: the decrease your expenses, the extra you could upload on your financial savings and investments.

1) Budgeting helps you control your spending

Everyone has a few terrible cash habits. Maybe you splurge on high-priced stuff you virtually don't need. You would possibly crave a flat white each morning and nip out to the neighborhood café and guiltily pay four dollars in place of making use of the loose stuff inside the smoko room. Whatever the horrific habit, budgeting allows you to control your spending better. If you've been given dreams in mind, a price range allows you to spot how small fees upload up and forestall you from accomplishing them. Seeing your desires slip similarly away, one espresso and scone at a time, maybe a superb motivator.

2. Budgeting enables you to place and gain your dreams in life whether it's travel, a lush

retirement, a pool, a boat, or perhaps simply having the ability to make your payments auto-pay, snug understanding there's sufficient cash to cover them, budgeting receives you there. Sitting down and honestly considering what you need in your life, then creating a price range to plot for it, enables you to get there faster.

3. Budgeting can help your married couples argue approximately money. But sitting down and getting ready for finance collectively helps you each understand your financial situation and keeps you working together to achieve your goals. No more arguments. Well, no more arguments about money.

4. Budgeting stops you from feeling overwhelmed when

payments come due at once, if the refrigerator breaks down, or Christmas appears to manifest loads extra than it should, it's easy to feel overwhelmed. However, having a financial way may minimize the stress. You've been given savings, you've forecasted and deliberated for the upcoming bills, and there's not anything to be concerned about.

5. Budgeting stops you from spending cash you don't have.

There's something freeing about knowing exactly how much money you can spend. If you set your budget for two hundred dollars of discretionary spending each week, that's it. When you attain that limit, you're done. This makes it clean to mention no to yourself, or the kids. We don't have that cash however let's have a take a observe this subsequent week.

6. Budgeting stops you from buying things you don't need

The kids want that toy. (Note that word 'want'). You suppose you 'need' a brand new saw (it's less complicated to justify a 'need' isn't it). But your finances say you can't get both till the subsequent month. That's great, because in the interim you'll borrow your neighbor's saw, and your kids will forget all about that toy they claimed would complete their life forever and move on to the next thing. A budget helps to slow your spending down so that you're less likely to spend unnecessarily.

7. Budgeting gets you out of debt
Credit cards. Loans. Mortgages. Hire purchases. Buy now, pay later. Debt may be crippling, and

it's stressful. Having a price range facilitates you to repay the debts, which prevents you from making extra debt. If you understand precisely what you may come up with the money to spend, there's no unplanned debt, no hobby being paid to a person else, and that cash remains in your bank.

8. Budgeting means you're prepared for emergencies.

Life is full of disasters. Fridges break down. The car engine lights come on. Family members get sick. These things are 100% going to happen, and you need to be prepared for them. A budget that provides for these emergencies means you will have money set aside for them so that life's speed bumps don't derail you completely.

9. Budgeting saves you money

If you have goals, strategies, and plans for your money, you'll find saving money is loads easier. Many humans have issues saving their money. It may be hard to keep a few stages of the strength of will and now no longer purchase matters that come up with quick periods or on-the-spot pleasure. But budgeting enables you to preserve your eyes on the prize. It makes you accountable. It keeps you from making those silly decisions, like buying the expensive cheese or being lured in by a new t-shirt.

10. Budgeting guarantees a glad retirement.

Part of any budgeting communique consists of retirement savings. That's due to the fact you need to maintain on dwelling lifestyle when you clock off from work; now no longer simply sit at home eating two-minute noodles, too scared to turn on a heater in case your electricity bill skyrockets. You want to make certain you've got sufficient cash to stay an existence that's enjoyable. Budgeting enables you to gain that.

Different Budget Types

The general phrase for keeping an eye on expenses and adhering to budgetary limitations is budgeting. There exist various budgetary formats that might be employed based on one's circumstances. Base budgets, conventional budgets, activity-based budgeting, and kaizen budgets are a few examples.

Let's examine some of these budgets in more detail.

A.   Base Allocations

Base budgets are a simple kind of budget that is usually related to ongoing operations. These will be the organization's prepared breakdown of various income and outlays. These budgets, which push toward reducing every expense feasible, can be typical for companies having cash profits.

However, it's crucial to include the costs required to guarantee that the company continues on its current course in the future. Rather than emphasizing short-term projects, base budgets often concentrate on continuing running costs.

B.   Customary Budget

A traditional budget's primary goal and greatest benefit is simplicity. As the name implies, a traditional budget will only cover the most fundamental techniques. The reason traditional budgeting is so well-liked is that it saves time.

You can estimate how much you might need to spend if you can use an incremental approach. The overall goal is to reflect on your prior financial decisions and learn from them. After that, you can adjust as necessary for the future.

C.   Budgets based on zero

The zero-based budget, as its name suggests, is constructed entirely from scratch. It doesn't account for prior experiences. This helps an organization   discover innovative methods for completing particular tasks. Using zero-based budgeting, funds are distributed according to how well-run various initiatives are.

It does not take past budgetary history into account. This implies that you have to justify and account for the various expenses for every new budgetary period.

D. Budget Kaizen

A kaizen budget entails routinely enhancing your procedures to assist in lowering various expenditures. This kind of budget, when made and followed, contributes to long-term gains. In most cases, you would include the anticipated cost savings in the budget itself.

This method of budgeting lowers overall expenses. However, a lot of planning is necessary. The largest problem, though, is that some improvements might occur sooner than the budget allows.

E. Budgets Based on Activities.

Using an activity-based budgeting approach is a comprehensive and efficient means of allocating expenses. The management may examine the expenses incurred and make an effort to find ways to cut them. This can be accomplished by reducing or even eliminating specific activity levels.

Increasing profitability is one of the main reasons a company might employ an activity-based budget. If the company doesn't have access to previous cost data, this strategy might be rather effective. Finally, you may examine all of the expenses related to each operational activity. You can identify which ones are reducing profits and change them as necessary.

F. Budgeting helps you succeed.

Budgeting helps you go forward by keeping your money on track and letting you know where you are. When done correctly, living paycheck to paycheck is eliminated. When you need money, you have it in the bank, a safety net for emergencies, and plans for the things you desire in life.

You can accelerate the accumulation of wealth by determining and eliminating wasteful and preventable expenses. It's that easy.

4. Maintain adequate insurance coverage without going overboard *(this is the continuation of Ways to Make Money out of Nothing)*

Insurance is a necessary expense that you should include in your budget. By getting insurance for both you and your primary assets—cars, homes, etc.—you can avoid suffering significant losses in the event of unfavorable circumstances.

You should, at the very least, get health insurance to protect yourself financially in the unlikely event that you contract an expensive illness. If you don't already have one, choose the best health insurance plan for you by researching and comparing options in the United Arab Emirates.

Think about homeowner and auto insurance if you own a home and a vehicle. In addition, you should think about getting term life insurance if you have dependent family members and children.

Building wealth is nice, but losing it to unanticipated situations or occurrences will be agonizing. Thus, take the initiative and protect the items that are most important to you.

Don't overinsure, though. There are plenty of worthless insurance products on the market. If there isn't a compelling need to acquire additional, stick to the four mentioned above.

According to Jack Ma, the richest man in China and the founder of Alibaba, "buying insurance does not change your life; it prevents your life from being changed."Purchasing coverage might not make you bankrupt, however no longer shopping for it's going to make your family bankrupt.

5. Make "extreme" financial sacrifices from your salary.

Although the 50:30:20 guideline is an excellent place to start, you'll discover that if you put in the effort, you may save a lot more.

There are going to be a lot of things in your budget that you may eliminate or decrease once you commit to building wealth. In doing so, you won't be by yourself. Communities that encourage "extreme" savings techniques are abundant these days.

The most well-known is the FIRE movement, which stands for "Financial Independence, Retire Early.

They urge followers to save an enormous portion of their monthly income by promoting "extreme" savings methods.

One of the pioneers of the FIRE movement, Jacob Lunk Fisker, advocated and followed a method that involved investing 60% to 80% of one's monthly income. At the age of 33, Fisker decided to retire, and he currently makes $7,000 a year living outside of Chicago.

Based on their personal finance experiments, which have shown them how to reduce spending and the consumerism that drives them up, Fisker and other leaders in the FIRE movement have built sizable networks.

They accomplish this in a variety of ways, such as by building and creating the items they require, such as tables instead of always purchasing them or bread. Fisker receives a sense of accomplishment in addition to money gains, which he considers more fulfilling than materialism.

Although saving 60% to 80% of your salary may seem an ambitious target for the time being, it at least shows you that there are plenty of ways to reduce your spending that you have probably not yet looked into.

Here are a few easy strategies to save costs and increase your savings in Dubai:

Make as many meals at home as you can, and shop for groceries in bulk.

Use filters on food delivery apps and cut down on restaurant spending to take advantage of different discounts.

To save money on energy costs, raise the temperature in your home by one degree.

Select a home exercise regimen.

Purchase specialty items such as TVs, refrigerators, and PCs at the Dubai Shopping Festival or GITEX.

Renegotiate your rent or look for better offers if it's more than 30% of your income, or more than

10% to 15% if you wish to follow Jacob Fisker.

Renew your mortgage's interest rate.

A comprehensive breakdown of the aforementioned ideas can be found in the article "12 Hacks for How to Save Money in Dubai Like a Resident"

Utilize these suggestions to raise your investable funds above the typical 20% of your income.

maintain in mind that what matters is how much you maintain, not how much you make.

And if you believe that being frugal is confining, consider what Amazon founder Jeff Bezos said: "I think frugalness fosters invention, just like other restraints do. Creating your escape is one of the only ways to get out of a tight spot.

6. Establish a savings account

Establishing an emergency fund is the next step in creating money from nothing after learning how to save a sizable portion of your income.

A self-funded emergency fund is similar to insurance. It's money placed aside for unanticipated events like job loss or lockdowns brought on by pandemics, as well as unforeseen costs like auto repairs.

Taking on debt and/or liquidating your investments are two methods to exacerbate unforeseen costs and circumstances.

You must pay interest on your loan, and when you sell your investments, you forfeit the amount you sold as well as whatever money they may have accrued from their exposure to the market had you stayed the course.

Thus, we advise you to learn how to establish an emergency fund as soon as possible to prevent those two situations. Three to six months' worth of costs should be saved up for emergencies. Additionally, make sure the money is in a savings account that you can quickly access in case you need it.

An emergency fund, like insurance, won't make you rich, but it will keep you from losing your investments or going into debt in times of need.

7. Develop new abilities

Reducing spending or increasing income are the two strategies to build up your assets and savings. Although a lot of financial counselors concentrate on the former, the latter also has to be given equal consideration.

If you work, enhance your skill set by enrolling in specialized courses and devoting yourself to ongoing professional growth. You can increase your salary through promotions and better job offers from other organizations by honing your hard and soft abilities.

If you run a small business, you should give your clients greater value, devote more resources to innovation, and deepen your grasp of the market. You can raise your revenue and market share by doing this.

8. Consider passive earnings options.

In addition to raising the revenue from your employment or business, you should look into several passive income sources.

Chapter 4

What is passive income

Money generated with little to no paintings or dedication is called passive income. It is produced using resources or endeavors in which a person is not actively involved. Rental income, dividends from investments, royalties from music or books, and earnings from automated online businesses are typical examples. While they frequently need an initial outlay of resources in the form of time, money, or effort to set up, passive income streams can offer financial security.

Passive income, in its strictest sense, relates to income sources like stock dividends or rental property. However, the phrase is being used more and more to describe earnings from earlier efforts, such as affiliate marketing commissions from a website you developed or royalties on original content.

The majority of passive income concepts need a lot of work upfront to generate continuous income.

You may increase your income and gain greater financial independence by incorporating passive income streams into your life.

One of the greatest passive income strategies is dropshipping, which allows you to work from anywhere.

Although it won't make you instantly wealthy, passive income presents chances to increase your income with little work.

Take a look at these passive income suggestions to make more money and create a more stable financial portfolio.

Entrepreneurs and creatives can earn more without working long hours with the help of low-input income opportunities like those on this list. The most effective passive income concepts keep making money even after you stop working for them.

1. Open a store that drops off goods

If your initial cash flow is poor, dropshipping is one of the greatest passive income ideas to earn money from anywhere. The dropshipping enterprise method includes putting in place an internet keep in which customers can discover and buy goods. Dropshipping is an intriguing business model since it eliminates the need for you to physically oversee or handle the things you sell.

Dropshipping allows your supplier to take care of all the manufacturing, packing, and fulfillment. Additionally, there is less capital risk associated with this passive income business because you don't have to pay your provider until your clients do. You can find popular products in many areas to offer in your store by using a platform such as DSers.

2 . Establish a print-on-call for business.

Print-on-demand is a good way to commercialize your creativity if you're an entrepreneur, designer, or artist. It entails collaborating with suppliers to personalize white-label goods like books, t-shirts, backpacks, and posters so that they can be sold individually. You simply have to pay for the product when you sell it, much like dropshipping. Neither inventory nor large purchases are required. Print-on-demand businesses make for a reliable source of passive revenue because You may produce goods rapidly and list them for sale in a matter of minutes.

Your supplier handles fulfillment and shipping. You may also automate some of your advertising and income tactics as soon as your keep is about up.

Producing goods for your Shopify business can be done fast and simply with the help of a print-on-demand provider like Printful. All things considered, print-on-demand is an easy-to-start, low-risk passive revenue stream.

3. Market digital goods

Digital products are assets or media that customers can't physically touch. These consist of files that may be streamed or downloaded, like PDFs, Kindle novels, templates, and plug-ins. Because digital items have large profit margins, they are excellent sources of revenue. The asset simply wishes to be created once, and you could promote it time and again via your online store. Neither inventory nor storage is required. You can promote as many virtual items as you like. By offering kits, printables, files, and other resources that are useful for professionals, many creators increase their passive income from digital assets.

4. Provide online education

Teachers now have an easier time than ever marketing courses online. You have a few regulations on how you may produce pre-recorded guides and start promoting them, whether or not your situation is marketing, illustration, or entrepreneurship. Without preserving any inventory or inventory, you could promote online guides regularly and make passive money.

There is an initial time commitment involved in teaching online. You must plan your course, record it, and produce digital materials, such as templates, that students may take with them. Regardless of your perspective, supplying online guides is an amazing approach to making money with little initial outlay of funds other than your time.

5. Start a blog.

Although starting a blog can be difficult, blogging as a passive income source is getting more and more popular.

Building a blog requires some time investment. However, if you produce high-quality material and market it on your channels, you'll grow a following large enough to bring in a sizable income.

You could use blogging to generate passive revenue by:

-Promoting affiliate goods

-Making sponsored content

-Promoting your goods

using Google AdSense to run advertisements

What's best? To launch a blog, you don't need any coding or design experience. You can quickly launch a blog with a content management system and hosting provider like Shopify.

6. Market homemade products

You can sell in hundreds of online stores. Some let you sell anything you desire, while others have specific niches like video games or artisan goods.

Among the well-known websites for internet sales are:

-Faire eBay, Amazon,

-AliExpress Ruby Lane

There are two upfront costs. To create and market handmade goods like ceramics or clothes, you'll need to make time and material investments. Additionally, you should set up an online shop to hold your goods.

You may build a brand for yourself and cut down on the amount of fees you pay on each sale by selling from your store. As you expand your audience and establish more connections with clients, the advantages of brand development multiply with time. It will eventually enable you to sell more and generate income online.

7. Manage a community of affiliates whose product or

service is recommended to an audience as part of affiliate marketing.

You get paid a commission each time a customer uses your referral link to purchase the suggested good or service, making it an excellent passive income option. There are several main reasons why Internet business owners become affiliate marketers:

It is simple to carry out. All you have to do is take care of the marketing aspect. The company will create goods and process orders.

Low risk applies. Joining an associate software is free. You don't need to invest any money upfront to sell existing gains.

It can be scaled. Most affiliate marketers don't employ additional staff. While your earlier paintings generate earnings inside the background, you could gift new merchandise to a target market and layout campaigns.

Making money with affiliate marketing can be a fulfilling method to expand your company's revenue sources. Your time is the simplest expense. After putting in the time, the benefits are cumulative.

8. Make online stock photo sales

Since photography is a service-based industry, unlike many other passive income suggestions on our list, you are usually compensated for your time. To make cash with photography, you have to be gifted at an occasion or photograph shoot, which may get tiresome after some time although you are making a fortune.

On the other hand, selling photographs online is a passive way to make money from photography if you're a full-time photographer or have a decent camera. High-quality images and videos can be purchased from stock photo websites such as Pexels, Shutterstock, and other online media outlets.

Shutterstock Stock photography website featuring an ocean

background image and search bar on the homepage.

You can easily integrate digital goods like prints or print-on-demand items like shirts and hats into your Shopify-powered photography business to create even more passive income streams that will allow you to work less and earn more money.

9. To Become an influencer on social media

You need to create a community of people who have similar interests to become a social media influencer or someone who can influence the purchasing decisions of others.

Do you enjoy comic books? You can open an Instagram account and begin regularly posting about the newest Marvel and DC television programs. The equal holds actually when you have an ardor for sports, scuba diving, indoor design, or maybe simply widespread culture.

You can use the engagement of your audience to support a number of different ideas for passive income. For example, you can collaborate with both big and small companies to market their goods to your audience.

Alternatively, you can profit by selling your merchandise.

10. Invest in a rental home

Investing in real estate is among the most traditional methods of accumulating passive income and long-term wealth.

If you have enough cash, you can purchase real estate, such as apartment buildings, and rent them out for rental income.

However, since managing tenants, maintaining properties, and collecting rent on a monthly basis are all part of the job description of a landlord, you can employ property managers to handle these tasks.

As the housing market improves, your properties will also appreciate, which will boost your profits if you decide to sell them in the future.

11. Make inventory marketplace investments

The stock market is a great way to create lasting wealth, despite the steep learning curve and potential for confusion. Thinking in the short term rather than taking a long view to achieve financial objectives is a common error that most people make when investing money.

Stock investments are intended to diversify your portfolio and lower risk. Investing in mutual funds, index funds, exchange-traded funds (ETFs), and high-dividend stocks that yield capital gains over time are some ways to achieve this.

S&P 500 graph illustrating gains and losses over time.

You must fund and open a brokerage account at a reputable

financial institution to begin investing in the stock market. It is advised that you consult a financial advisor as well to plan and achieve the objectives of your passive income strategy.

12. Let your extra room be rented

Perhaps you lack the preliminary investment important to put money into condominium properties. However, do you have a spare room in your flat? Or do you want to avoid leaving your house empty while you go on a three-week road trip? You can list your available space for rent by collaborating with a rental company such as VRBO or Airbnb.

Homeowners and travelers who are looking for their next getaway can connect through Airbnb. Because Airbnb is frequently more convenient and occasionally less expensive than hotels, there is a high demand for your available space as an Airbnb host.

It's possible to generate passive income by renting out one extra room, but it's better to rent out ten. Depending on local laws, you may be able to purchase apartments solely for the purpose of renting them out if you want to increase your Airbnb income. However, keep in mind that renting out your space frequently involves upfront work. Before listing your space for rent, you might need to remodel or furnish it.

13. Take a car rental

You can rent out other items in addition to your house to generate passive income. Using a provider like Turo, you could additionally lease out your vehicle. If you already drive for Uber or Carvertise, you can register with these platforms to make additional money while you travel around the city.

Finding someone who needs a car for Uber or Lyft is another way to make money with your vehicle. Hence, while your car works for you, you can watch a Netflix show in your spare time rather than go for a drive.

14. Give money to colleagues

Have extra money lying around that's not helping you? As a side gig, consider peer-to-peer lending. The lending of money to borrowers or small businesses is known as peer-to-peer lending.

You can register on a website that links borrowers and lenders, such as LendingClub, Prosper (for individuals), or Worthy (for businesses), to make the process simple.

Typically, loan requests and interest rates based on the borrower's past are hosted on these websites. These loans typically yield returns of between 5% and 6%. Your cash flow will be higher as you lend more money.

15. Make money while you shop online

When you shop online, cashback reward sites like Swagbucks, MyPoint, and Rakuten let you make passive income. You only need to shop on these websites after signing up to earn money from them. You earn more points the more you shop online. and the higher your earning potential.

A word of caution: avoid going over your credit limit or maxing out your credit card in an attempt to get rewarded.

16. Purchase and sell domains

There are websites available on almost any subject you can imagine. What's best? Many of them generate substantial incomes from sources like affiliate marketing, advertising, paid memberships, or products; they are frequently offered for sale.

After creating and validating an account, websites such as BizBuySell facilitate the safe purchase and sale of virtual stores.

It's a fantastic way to run a company if you already have some customers and traffic. After completing your purchase, you will also have access to seller support to make sure everything goes smoothly.

17. Launch a channel on YouTube

You can still launch a YouTube channel. Every month, a staggering 2.7 billion people use YouTube worldwide. It would take a lot of eyes to generate that kind of passive income. The drawback? In the beginning, there is little to no return on the extensive upfront work.

However, if you're willing to put in a lot of upfront work and have a long-term outlook, having a successful YouTube channel has a big earning potential. As your audience grows and you accumulate content, clicks, and views, you can earn passive income through affiliate sales, sponsorships, branded integrations, and ad revenue. Even more readily

branch out to launch a podcast and increase your revenue through sponsorships.

18. Purchase REITs

What if you lack the funds to purchase entire apartment complexes? Is rental income still an option for you? You can, indeed.

Using a real estate investment trust (REIT) platform such as Fundrise, you can invest with a $500 minimum and purchase a range of real estate assets, which will increase in value over time and provide you with more passive income. A business that owns and operates profitable real estate is known as a REIT. Smaller investors can pool their funds in this way to make investments that they otherwise couldn't afford.

If you have some startup capital, one of the best income ideas to consider as a long-term investment is real estate investment trusts. Starting a business requires both upfront cash and extensive research. You shouldn't enter into this investment mindlessly. Fortunately, there are lots of tools available to assist you in getting started, such as this guide.

19. Online design sales

Selling digital designs online on websites like 99designs, ThemeForest, or Creative Market is a fantastic way to start a side income. These platforms offer a built-in market that is already looking for design resources, regardless of whether you use them to create website themes, logos, branding resources, templates, illustrations, or even fonts.

Creative Market's homepage features a collage of various examples of its websites.

For example, you would have to apply and wait for approval if you wanted to start selling designs on Creative Market. From there, you obtain your own retail space where you can begin offering your distinctive designs for sale.

20. Make business investments

It is now very possible to begin investing in business opportunities that were previously unattainable. With a $100 initial investment and no investor fees, platforms like Mainvest make it simple to invest passively.

The yields? Like any other investment, it's contingent. However, Mainvest wants to pay you between 10% and 25%. You are not even required to personally inspect the companies. Mainvest handles the screening procedure on your behalf. All you have to do to get started is invest the money.

This is a fantastic, risk-free way to start investing in businesses as a passive income option and gain experience along the way.

21. Let out any extra space you have.

Do you have an unfinished garage or basement? Rent out the gap for storage! This can be accomplished effectively and safely with storage rental platforms such as:

Peerspace   StoreAtMyHouse
Neighbor

By 2026, the storage market is expected to reach a value of up to $64 billion. Put differently, this is not a revenue stream that will disappear anytime soon. Among the things you can store are automobiles, boats, recreational vehicles, and even stock for a business.

Using storage rental platforms is a great way to reduce liability risks because those systems provide steady charge methods, contracts, and consumer and garage issuer information.

22. Establish a job posting

A job board is a fantastic way for an online entrepreneur to generate passive income. Employers put up for sale task openings on those websites to task seekers.

Both online and offline job searches are options for job seekers. Employers can pay to post jobs on your job board, and you can charge for additional features like sponsored jobs or unrestricted access to your applicant pool.

You can start making passive income right away by purchasing a job board theme if you don't want to create a job board from scratch. Now, the simple part is creating the website. The majority of your work is in making people aware of your job board.

You can anticipate a sizable portion of your revenue being passive once you start the flywheel and your job board starts to attract repeat users. For inspiration, visit websites like

ProBlogger, Dribble, or Construction Jobs.

23. Make apps without coding

Amazingly, today's no-code tools allow even non-programmers to create basic to complex mobile applications. Start-up platforms such as Adalo, Bubble, and Appy Pie make this feasible.

You must first choose between developing a mobile app and a

website. In addition to the app's concept (i.e., the problem it will solve and the niche it will serve), monetization is another important consideration.

Via a mobile app, you can make passive income by doing the following:

-Ads for Subscriptions

-To download, pay

-An approach to the market

There is a great list of research tools here to help you figure out what problem your app should solve if you are unsure.

You can learn which keywords have a high search volume by using Ubersuggest.

After that, all you need to do is set up your digital guide to start receiving sales, either via a seller platform or your storefront.

24. Earn royalties from your inventions

Inventors are still around today. Your original inventions can generate passive income. Although it's not a commonly discussed passive income stream, this one exists.

One of the most challenging aspects of the journey of the inventor is likely getting started. Make sure your invention is worthwhile, practical, and addresses a need. To begin, check the US patent website to make sure your concept hasn't been thought of before.

Websites like Invention City can assist you in getting started if you wish to sell your invention outright. Once your idea is on the market, you may be able to passively earn a percentage or payouts from the revenue it generates, depending on the terms of the agreement you reach.

25. Set audiobooks to record

Someone has to produce audiobooks. Why can't you be that person? Once you get into the business, royalties—which are how most audiobook narrators are compensated—can be a source of passive income.

There are a few things you must first master if you want to profit from audiobooks. Among these is education:

-ways to audition

-Appropriate storytelling methods

-Which specialty do you pursue

-A few editing abilities

You don't need to tackle it by yourself. It's simpler to get started and get your first few gigs on some platforms. Visit websites such as ACX to find out what is required to succeed in the field.

26. Get a vending machine investment

Ever marvel who continues all the one's always-stocked merchandising machines? Your cravings for soda and snacks are generating (semi) passive income for the owner of those machines.

Vending machines do require an initial time and financial investment to get started as a passive source of income. This is an excellent guide that offers advice on how to set up your first vending machine.

You can estimate the initial investment you'll need to make to buy your first set of machines (as well as how many you can afford to start with) by using marketplaces like Craigslist, eBay, and BizBuySell. A vending machine route is a great cash-flowing source of mostly passive income once you secure locations where you can install them.

27. Create and marketplace spreadsheets

A few of us are naturally skilled at spreadsheets. If that describes you, you could use your proficiency with spreadsheets to generate passive income.

There is a market that will pay you to create spreadsheets for a variety of uses, such as budgeting, profit projections, habit tracking, or even P&L spreadsheets that business owners don't want to create from scratch. You can use Excel or Google Sheets for this work.

When you combine the Digital Downloads app with a Shopify storefront, you'll have a ready-to-pay passive income stream. However, for that to occur, you do need to draw customers to your storefront. Thankfully, we have some tools at our disposal.

28. Open a high-yield savings account

By paying out more interest than standard savings accounts, high-yield accounts produce passive income. You gradually earn interest by making deposits into this account without putting in extra effort. Over 4% APY is offered by certain high-yield savings accounts and certificates of deposit.

Essentially, this interest is "free money" that builds up as your savings increase. For novices looking to begin generating income and accumulating wealth, high-yield savings accounts provide a secure, low-risk alternative, despite the possibility of lower returns than other investments.

29. Charge a parking space rental

With little work, renting out vacant parking spots can bring in passive income. You can make money off of the vacant space by advertising locally or by listing your available spot on a parking-sharing platform.

You will benefit financially while renters who want convenient parking will pay a fee, generating a low-maintenance, consistent stream of income.

Choose the best passive income strategy for you.

There's only so much time in a day, so figuring out how to make a lot of money more quickly can help you reach your financial goals by giving you financial flexibility. Whatever that level is—it could be going on a fantastic trip or getting that amazing pair of shoes—adding passive income streams with distinct underlying economics can

allow you the flexibility to pursue
it.

Chapter 5

What makes passive income so crucial?

It's critical to have passive income for various reasons.

1.Financial Stability and Security: Even in the event that your main source of income is lost, passive income offers a consistent flow of cash.

2.Time Freedom: By earning money with little effort on your part, passive income enables you to devote more of your time to other interests, like traveling, pursuing hobbies, or spending time with family.

3.Building Wealth: One important component of wealth building may be passive income. It gives you the tools to invest and save, enabling your money to increase over time.

4.Diversification: It can be dangerous to rely only on active income. By diversifying your sources of income, passive income lessens your reliance on a single job or line of business.

5.Retirement Planning: By providing a steady stream of income without requiring active work during your retirement years, passive income can support your retirement.

6.Entrepreneurship: Passive income models can give entrepreneurs a more secure financial base, allowing them to explore new business opportunities or make investments to expand their companies.

7.Financial Freedom: In the end, having several passive income sources can help you achieve financial freedom, which gives you the freedom to live your life as you see fit and to choose whether or not to work.

It's crucial to remember that even though passive income has many advantages, setting up the income streams frequently calls for initial effort, commitment, and hard work.

Chapter 6

Wealth preservation: Crucial tactics for preserving and safeguarding your wealth

Since you've worked hard to increase your wealth, you should always put protecting it first. But in the current economic climate, it might seem particularly difficult. An extensive financial plan should be in place now more than ever with interest rates rising, volatile markets, and general economic uncertainty.

According to Russell St. John, a wealth management advisor for U.S.Bancorp Investments, "volatility inside the markets and the area is the use of humans to are trying to find havens. It takes a combination of tactics to protect your wealth. These six strategies, which include a well-funded savings account, a diversified investment portfolio, and insurance, could help you maintain your wealth in a difficult economic climate when used collectively.

1.   Establish a budget to safeguard family assets
Everything starts with a plan. A qualified financial expert can assist you in determining your objectives and making recommendations for steps to take to achieve them.

According to St. John, "My job is to find out where my clients are financially right now and where they want to be in the future. The person might declare, 'I have to pay my bills today, but my wish is to buy a house on a lake or leave assets to my favorite charity.' A plan is based on where those two things intersect.

Spend some time reviewing your financial plan, if you have one in place already. It's critical to adapt your plan as you get older and as your circumstances change. Young people have plenty of time and don't need to worry as much about volatility, according to St. John. Your assets, however, need more protection as you approach retirement.

2. Establish emergency or major purchase savings to safeguard family wealth

You can better manage unforeseen events and your daily cash flow by setting aside money for emergencies or future expenses. Financial experts frequently advise saving up to three to six months' worth of expenses so you won't have to prematurely access funds from a retirement account or certificate of deposit (CD).

According to St. John, there are risks that you can control and risks that you can't. We are able to modify your portfolio according to your risk tolerance; however, we have no control over an unexpected medical bill or the breakdown of your furnace.

3. To protect your wealth, diversify your investment portfolio.

It can be beneficial to have tools in your portfolio that "zig" while others "zag" to lessen the effects of market volatility. According to St. John, diversification can be beneficial on a number of levels and refers to the practice of not placing all of your money in investments belonging to the same risk class. "Within bonds, for example, you can diversify all through kinds of bonds or industries," the author claims. You could purchase products from the banking sector, the technology sector, and the industrial sector. Not all of your investments will be affected by a specific sector of the economy's weakness.

Diversification also guards against the risk of concentration. If you invest half of your money in the stock of your company, for instance, your retirement funds may be at risk if the stock falls.

4. Invest in life, disability, and long-term care insurance to safeguard family wealth. These

policies can shield your assets from unforeseen changes to your profession, family, or health. Traditionally, human beings have the idea of coverage as a manner to shield their families, and that makes more sense when you're young and term life insurance is cheap," says St. John. "

Some, for instance, also can be implemented in long-term period care. According to St.John, "You could use the coins cost for that in case you want the cash at some stage in retirement. "If you die, your family will be taken care of. Additionally, your family won't have to worry about paying for long-term care support if you end up needing it because you have a plan in place.

5. Use tax planning to protect your wealth

The procedure of putting in place your monetary affairs to lessen your tax legal responsibility is called tax planning. To lawfully optimize your tax situation, entails making smart judgments regarding your income, investments, and spending. By maximizing deductions, utilizing available tax credits, and lowering their tax burden, individuals and businesses can benefit from effective tax planning. To make wise financial decisions that can result in large savings, tax rules and regulations usually need to be carefully considered.

Tax-making plans are vital for some reasons.

Minimizing Tax Liability: You may lawfully minimize your tax liability by keeping your finances in order. This will give you more money to save, invest, or spend.

Choosing tax-efficient investment options is one way that tax planning helps you optimize your investments so that they grow with the least amount of tax consequences on returns.

Maximizing Deductions: With careful planning, you can minimize your taxable income and your tax payment by utilizing all of the available credits, exemptions, and deductions.

Avoiding fines: Being aware of tax regulations will help you steer clear of expensive errors and fines that may result from incomplete or inaccurate filings.

Future Planning: For long-term financial objectives like retirement and estate planning, effective tax planning is crucial. It guarantees that your assets are safeguarded and effectively transferred to your heirs.

Compliance and Peace of Mind: You can have peace of mind knowing that your financial affairs are in order and that tax-related stress is minimized by adhering to tax rules.

Business Success: Tax planning is essential to a company's capacity to turn a profit. It supports cost optimization, cash flow management, and maintaining market competitiveness.

All things considered, tax preparation is a proactive strategy that can result in major short- and long-term savings as well as financial security.

6.   Create an estate plan to safeguard family assets and leave a legacy.

To protect your fortune for your family and the causes you care about, you can utilize a trust, a will, and other legal documents. A will might be appropriate for families with modest assets. However, it's crucial to see an estate planning lawyer if your family has more complicated needs, you own a business, or you own investment property.

Invest sensibly by spreading your money over a variety of asset classes, such as mutual funds, equities, bonds, and real estate. Your belongings can also additionally land up in probate and the courts can also additionally determine wherein they move in case your property plan is not in reality defined," warns St. John. Additionally, estate planning can assist with asset transfers and taxes.

- Budgeting: Make a thorough budget that lists all of your sources of income and expenses. Review it often and make any necessary adjustments.

- Emergency Fund: To prepare for unforeseen financial difficulties, keep an emergency fund equal to three to six months' worth of living expenses.

Invest in a variety of assets to spread your money around and lower your risk. Always adjust your investment holdings.

- Track Expenses: Be mindful of your spending patterns and eliminate wasteful spending.

- Constant Learning: Through books, courses, and seminars, stay up to date on investment methods and financial trends.

- Tax Efficiency: Make the most of your investments to minimize taxes. Employ tax-sheltered savings plans and offsets.

- Professional Advice: For individualized wealth management plans, speak with financial advisors and specialists.

- Insurance Coverage: Make sure your life, health, property, and other assets are adequately covered by insurance.

- Reduce Debt: Pay off high-interest loans and reduce your overall debt. Utilize credit sensibly.

- Regular Contributions: For compound growth, make regular contributions to your mutual funds and retirement accounts.

- Reinvestment: To enable your investments to grow

enormously, reinvest interest and dividends.

- Evaluate Investments: Analyze your investments' performance regularly and make any necessary adjustments in light of the state of the market.

- Legal Protection: Use legal tools like estate planning, trusts, and wills to protect your wealth.

- Keep Up: Stay informed on world events and economic news that could affect your assets.

- Make Reasonable Financial Decisions: Steer clear of rash investments and big-ticket purchases.

Always bargain for better terms when making investments, hiring services, or making purchases.

- Network: To take advantage of future commercial

prospects and joint ventures, keep up a robust professional network.

- Health & Wellness: Make an investment in your well-being; over time, preventive treatment can significantly reduce medical expenses.

- Frequent Exercise: Maintaining long-term wealth can be aided by regular physical activity, which also lowers stress and medical expenses.

Spending with mindfulness means choosing carefully what you buy and staying away from unnecessary spending.

- Savings Practices: Even in times of economic prosperity, maintain regular savings practices.

- Property upkeep: Keep your properties in good condition to avoid future expensive repairs and to preserve their worth.

- Review Subscriptions: Get rid of any unneeded or superfluous subscriptions and services by periodically reviewing them.

- Invest in abilities: To increase your income potential and job stability, keep improving your abilities.

- Family Communication: Make sure all members of your family are in agreement on your financial objectives by including them in financial conversations.

- Avoid Speculation: Steer clear of speculative investments that have a high chance of losing a lot of money.

Review your financial objectives on a regular basis, and make any adjustments to your methods.

- Philanthropy: As a way to promote a sense of fulfillment and a beneficial impact on the community, think about giving back to society through charitable donations.
- Make a Retirement Plan: Make regular contributions to retirement accounts to

guarantee a pleasant retirement.

- Regular Assessments: To find possible areas for improvement, periodically have professionals evaluate your financial health.

In the rapidly changing economic climate of today, it is more crucial than ever to be proactive and protect your financial stability. In these unpredictable times, securing and increasing personal wealth is of utmost importance. This book explores a wide range of practical and dependable techniques that can help people build stronger financial foundations, make the most of their assets, and create the conditions for long-term success.

Conclusion:

Maintaining and increasing one's own wealth is a journey that calls for careful preparation and wise choices. By putting these tactics into practice, you can build a solid financial foundation, manage debt well, and protect your possessions. With discipline, patience, and a proactive attitude to financial management, wealth preservation and growth are possible.